REAL ESTATE
LOUISE PAGE

A Methuen New Theatrescript
Methuen · London and New York

Also by Louise Page
BEAUTY AND THE BEAST (forthcoming)
GOLDEN GIRLS
SALONIKA

ESSEX COUNTY LIBRARY

A METHUEN PAPERBACK

First published in Great Britain as a Methuen Paperback original in 1985 by
Methuen London Ltd, 11 New Fetter Lane, London EC4P 4EE
and in the United States of America by
Methuen Inc, 733 Third Avenue, New York, NY 10017

British Library Cataloguing in Publication Data
Page, Louise
    Real estate.
    I. Title
    822'.914   PR6066.A3/

    ISBN 0 413 57950 6

Printed in Great Britain by Expression Printers Ltd, London N7

CAUTION

To Philip, Kate, Martha and Chloe

Real Estate was first performed at the Tricycle Theatre, London on 3 May 1984, with the following cast:

GWEN	Brenda Bruce
JENNY	Charlotte Cornwell
DICK	Glyn Owen
ERIC	Tony Guilfoyle

Directed by Pip Broughton
Designed by Ellen Cairns
Lighting by Andy Phillips

ACT ONE

Scene One

The wood at the back of a house.
It is autumn – late dusk.
Dead leaves.
A ball crosses the stage.

GWEN (*off*): Cleo!

Enter GWEN. She carries a dog lead. She rattles the lead. She whistles.

Cleo! Cleo! You naughty girl!

She waits for the dog. She shouts off stage.

Thank you. She always goes back to the house when we get this far.

She waits. She picks up an acorn. The acorn has a small root and has leaves and mud round it.
Enter JENNY. She is holding the ball. She is dressed almost identically to GWEN except that she is wearing silly shoes.

I never seem to go home without something in my pocket. The next time I find them they're withered.

JENNY: You should empty your pocket.

GWEN: Yes.

She throws the acorn away.

Cleo! Cleo! Samba died. Well put down. You don't expect dogs to last for ever do you? This one's called Cleo. Dick's choice. I couldn't do all the naming of them.

JENNY: No.

GWEN: Dick's dog more than mine really. Spends most of the day with him. It doesn't feel safe now to walk in these woods without some sort of companion.

JENNY: The same everywhere.

GWEN: Worse in towns I expect.

JENNY: I have a car.

GWEN: Oh.

JENNY: And a flat. Two bedrooms. Second floor.

GWEN: Where?

JENNY: London. Hammersmith.

GWEN: Oh.

JENNY: There's a view of the river from the balcony.

GWEN: I see.

JENNY tries to get some leaves from her shoe.

JENNY: Silly shoes for here.

GWEN: At least it's not wet.

JENNY: No.

GWEN: Did you drive in them?

JENNY: Yes.

GWEN: How long did it take?

JENNY: An hour and a half. Longer than it should. The traffic was choc-a-bloc coming out of London.

GWEN: I always go by train.

JENNY: I assumed the station would be closed by now.

GWEN: It is. Dick drives me to Didcot. You could have been collected.

JENNY: I didn't want to be a nuisance.

She holds out the ball.

GWEN: You still bite your nails.

JENNY: Yes.

GWEN: Most people grow out of it.

JENNY: I have tried. It was either this or smoking.

GWEN: I smoke.

JENNY: You shouldn't.

GWEN: You tell me that?

JENNY: Anybody would.

GWEN: It's my own life! I throw it away as I please.

Pause.
DICK calls from the house.

DICK: Gwen. Gwenny?

GWEN: Dick's waiting for me.

Pause.

Am I supposed to say something? Well? What did you expect?

JENNY shakes her head.

DICK (*off*): Gwen!

GWEN: I'm here. (*To* JENNY.) I can't ask

you to stay for supper because I don't know if there's enough. Are you expecting to be asked to stay? Dick's province not mine. He's the one who knows how long the mince has been in the freezer. How many sheets there are which haven't been turned edge to edge. Don't think we can't afford new sheets. We can, easily. It's just we prefer them to be linen and at our – that's what we prefer.

DICK (*off*): Gwen?

GWEN: It's not fair to keep him waiting –

> GWEN *starts to go.*

JENNY: There are some questions –

GWEN: There had to be something.

JENNY: Why?

GWEN: Why else would you come?

> *They are very still.*

It's not intuition. I'd assumed it would be money. It obviously isn't. I know how much Jaeger suits cost.

> JENNY *laughs.*

This is my money. Not Dick's. Dick's as well as mine of course. I'm the one that works now.

JENNY: It suits you.

GWEN: Thank you.

> *Enter* DICK.

JENNY: Hello Dick.

DICK: Jenny!

GWEN: It took her an hour and a half to drive from London.

JENNY: The traffic was bad.

GWEN: Did Cleo come in?

DICK: I thought she was with you.

GWEN: No.

> GWEN *starts to move off stage.*

Cleo! You're a naughty girl. Cleo! Come back here this minute.

> *She has gone.*

DICK: How are you?

JENNY: Fine.

DICK: Good.

JENNY: And you?

DICK: Bearing up.

JENNY: I hear you do the cooking.

DICK: Gwen's at work all day. She doesn't have the time. It's not how I thought my retirement would be. All rather piecemeal.

JENNY: Housework is.

DICK: She's an estate agent, a good estate agent. The clients like her. She sells houses very successfully. She found it very exciting at first. I don't know now. It's her name you see on the boards. She earns more than I was earning. Perhaps you expected to find us struggling?

JENNY: I don't know.

DICK: On your way here you must have thought.

JENNY: I thought you'd be old. Older. You are of course. And me?

> *Pause.*
> DICK *watches her.*
> JENNY *bends down for an acorn. The gesture stops.*

Do I remind you of her?

DICK: Not particularly. No.

JENNY: Sometimes I think I am. It suddenly surprises me. Something I say. How I put my clothes in order in the drawers. The way I boil eggs.

DICK: It would be hard to better. Hers is a very reliable method.

JENNY: I've never compared it. The egg's just an example.

> *She throws the acorn away.*

I can't explain.

DICK: You live in London?

JENNY: Yes. I have a flat. Two bedrooms. Second floor. Hammersmith. There's a view of the river from the balcony.

DICK: I see. You aren't married?

JENNY: No and I haven't been. Did you think there'd be step-grandchildren somewhere?

DICK: We've thought a lot of things. You couldn't have expected us not to. How do you earn your living?

JENNY: I work in a shop. Not behind the

counter at Woolworth's as you promised me I would. More up market than that. You made the threat of working at Woolworth's sound terribly glamorous. Rather risque. The sort of place it would be fun to work. I buy china. I've quite an eye for it. I can see if a teapot's likely to pour well. I've just got a big firm to reappraise their glaze. It cracked in dishwashers. That's quite a major victory. And of course there have been other things on the way.

DICK: I look forward to hearing about them. Will you stay for supper?

JENNY: She said she didn't know if there'd be enough.

DICK: It'll stretch.

JENNY: If you're sure.

DICK: It's not the fatted calf.

JENNY: I didn't expect it to be. I should lock the car.

Exit JENNY.
DICK *watches her.*
Enter GWEN. *She wears an apron which is obviously his.*

GWEN: I've turned the sprouts down.

DICK: Thank you.

GWEN: Do you think she's attractive? She is, isn't she? More than I thought she would be. I suppose I thought she'd come back in denim and with beads. It all looks as if it's real gold. She is attractive, isn't she?

DICK: Well –

GWEN: How did you think she'd be? Tell me. I've thought so many things I don't know.

DICK: Gwenny –

GWEN: I'm all right. You'd think Christmas or a birthday. Even over a weekend. But Thursday?

DICK: Perhaps she's on her way somewhere.

GWEN: Just dropping in. Is that all?

DICK: She's having supper with us.

GWEN: I wonder if she would like to stay the night.

DICK: She might want to drive back. It's only ninety minutes.

GWEN: The spare bed isn't aired. I could put both hot water bottles in –

DICK: We might not want her to stay.

GWEN: Are sprouts a vegetable she liked? I don't remember. I know there's something she would never eat.

DICK: There are still runner beans. I'll do those.

Enter JENNY.

GWEN: Do you like brussel sprouts?

JENNY: Fine.

GWEN: What's the vegetable that you don't like?

JENNY: There isn't one I don't think.

GWEN: There was. You swore it made you sick. I thought it was a fad. I made soup with it and told you it was something different. You were sick.

JENNY: I'm not fond of turnip.

GWEN: No –

DICK: There are some beans from the garden in the freezer. I'll do those.

JENNY: I don't want to be any trouble.

GWEN: It'll come back to me.

DICK: Ten minutes.

Exit DICK.

JENNY: He looks very fit.

GWEN: He's not the sort of husband that has heart attacks. Not that you can ever say of course. It'll probably be me.

JENNY: Dick says you're a success.

GWEN: Just started as a hobby. It rather grew. We're not the biggest, not by any means. One branch that's all. We're not tied up to a building society either. The press is never good on estate agents but I like to think that I try. That I do care. Houses are about families aren't they? Will you stay the night?

JENNY *shrugs.*

It's just that beds need airing. That sort of thing.

JENNY: We might not like each other.

GWEN: I didn't mean it like that.

JENNY: But we mightn't.

GWEN: We can just talk. I'd like to hear about your life. You don't look as if things have gone badly for you.

JENNY: I suppose they haven't. Not if you treat them as a whole.

GWEN: I'm glad.

JENNY: This is all my own. I'm not married for it.

GWEN: You'd have a ring.

JENNY: And a diamond.

GWEN: Yes.

Pause.
JENNY starts to move towards the house.

JENNY: You've got a green house.

GWEN: Dick's domain not mine. He finally got aubergines to grow this year.

JENNY: Oh.

GWEN: You don't know for how long. They'd become an obsession. There's always something he can't get to grow. Disaster with the celery this year. It was supposed to be self-blanche – it was celery you didn't like. I said the soup was onion and I made croutons.

JENNY: I was sick?

GWEN: Yes.

JENNY: News to me.

GWEN: There are probably a lot of things.

JENNY: Yes, there are some questions.

GWEN: Are you pregnant?

JENNY: How?

GWEN: There are some questions and you bite your nails instead of smoking.

JENNY: Yes.

GWEN: And not married?

JENNY: Not living with anybody either.

GWEN: So it's help?

JENNY nods.

I'd have thought abortions were easier to get in London. But here? Can you pay?

They look at each other.

Oh. I'm supposed to congratulate you?

JENNY: I think so.

GWEN: Jenny. How long?

JENNY: Only just. Six weeks.

GWEN: October, no September, October, November, December –

JENNY: May. Around the twelfth at a rough estimate.

GWEN: You're lucky. It's hell being pregnant in the summer. My own fault for putting on so much weight with you. Is it those sort of questions?

JENNY: Yes. I need to know if I've had German measles. My friend – he had his daughter with him last weekend. Lottie had a temperature and a rash and they called the doctor. There's an epidemic at the moment.

GWEN: Your friend is married?

JENNY: Divorced. Not me. A long time before me. And we are friends. We go to bed together. You'd probably call that lovers. We aren't.

GWEN: You don't have to tell me about that side of things.

JENNY: I wanted to explain.

GWEN: And if you haven't had German measles.

JENNY: Then it'll have to be abortion. I need to know.

GWEN: And then you'll disappear again?

JENNY: Please mother.

GWEN: You have. And mumps and measles and chicken pox. All the usual vaccinations.

JENNY: Thank you.

GWEN: You see I thought I was probably a grandmother by now. A granny. In May.

JENNY: Probably. There are a lot of tests I have to have. I'm old for a child. It's becoming a classic syndrome according to the doctor. A woman who's worked and got somewhere and then panicked because she's never used her womb. Wanting to see it's operational before the guarantee runs out. It wasn't consciously like that. I've never played Vatican Roulette. On the pill, I never missed a pill. And I've never changed it even when I thought it was safe without a diaphragm. It wasn't even anything special. Between the sheets with the light off. Sleep afterwards and work in the morning. I suppose there are a lot of beginnings like that.

GWEN: Does he know?

JENNY: Not yet. When I went to the doctor's this morning he was still asleep. His arm was over the top of the duvet. He's got a ten year old daughter and I thought he didn't look old enough to be a father. He's younger than me. A couple of years that's all. You and Dick I suppose.

GWEN: Five between us. But I never say it. In the beginning it was a joke. But as you get older. You will tell your friend?

JENNY: Eric. Of course. I haven't been sick yet. Were you sick?

GWEN: Not as much as some people. I put on weight and my ankles swole. That was the worst –

DICK (*off*): White or red?

JENNY: I'm not drinking.

GWEN: Not fussy.

DICK (*off*): One minute and counting.

GWEN: On our way.

JENNY: Will you tell him?

GWEN: Not if you don't want me to.

JENNY *goes towards the house;* GWEN *follows her.*
    GWEN *stops to pick up the acorn she threw down before she stands.*
    The light goes out.

Scene Two

The house; DICK *and* JENNY. JENNY *is looking at the contents of the room.* DICK *is doing a large tapestry.*

JENNY: Samba?

DICK: Yes. Already an old dog when that was taken.

JENNY: None of me?

DICK: No.

JENNY: Nowhere?

DICK: Not that I know of.

JENNY: Where's this?

DICK: The first house she sold.

JENNY: Oh. There used to be one of me as a baby in this frame.

DICK: I don't know what happened to them. There wasn't a great gesture of burning or tearing up. Nothing like that. One by one they just disappeared. You can't blame us. There have been a lot of tears. A lot of pain.

He sews.

JENNY: Forgiveness is rather overrated as a quality.

DICK: You don't have to like me even now.

JENNY: I know that.

DICK: What else could I have done? You promised to be home at eleven. You weren't. Are you surprised we were worried? Eleven o'clock you'd given your word. We didn't know what might have happened to you. It was nearly two. You could have telephoned. Asked if you could stay a little longer. If you'd asked us we would have come to some arrangement with you. I could have come and collected you.

JENNY: You didn't want me to go in the first place did you?

DICK: No we didn't.

JENNY: You didn't or she didn't?

DICK: Neither of us thought it was a very good idea.

JENNY: You were the one who came and got me. I've never been so embarrassed.

DICK: Because I cared?

JENNY: No one else's father stormed in and played the heavy.

DICK: I'm not your father.

JENNY: That made it worse.

DICK: Let's get this straight, I knocked at the door and asked for you and they let me in. There was no storming. You were the one who screamed and said that you weren't coming home. Do you know what it took me to walk into that party? Into the noise. A dark room filled with smoke and Beatles music. I was frightened. It wasn't my territory. I'd have left you to come home when you liked. But Gwen asked me to. A test. Bare feet on broken glass. The part of her that nothing else could convince.

JENNY: Don't!

DICK: Jenny –

She struggles with the photo frame.

JENNY: Some people put the new ones in on top of the old. Eric does that with Lottie's. All her school photos, one on top of the other.

This is not the case.

DICK: I had to encourage her to forget you. It would have torn us apart Jenny. I couldn't have faced that. I could have gone so you'd come back, but if you went once you could go again. Then where would she have been? We had friends who wanted to move from a big house to a smaller one. And another set who wanted to do the opposite. I encouraged Gwen to introduce them to each other and to run around with tape measures. A deal was done. They insisted on giving her something for her trouble. I think it was twenty pounds. With that she went out and ordered headed notepaper and foolscap envelopes. She stopped being your mother and went into business. I pushed her at first and now I can't stop her.

JENNY: You don't like her working?

DICK: I took early retirement so we could spend some time together. I still want her Jenny. I want her to look back when she goes out of the house in the morning.

He drops his needle. JENNY *returns it to him.*

Thank you.

JENNY: It's very beautiful. I'm hopeless at anything like that. I can't even knit.

DICK: Perhaps you'd like it when it's finished.

JENNY: Me?

DICK: I could send it to you. It would mean leaving your address.

JENNY: I'd like that. Thank you.

She watches DICK *sew. Enter* GWEN.

GWEN: I've taken the risk on two hot water bottles and the electric blanket. I know you shouldn't combine electricity and water but I've done the stoppers as tight as I could.

JENNY: Thank you.

GWEN: Cleo's scratching at the door to go out.

DICK: I forgot. She's a dog of very regular habits. How far did you take her this afternoon?

GWEN: Only to the stream and back. She ought to have a bit of a run.

DICK: Right. Into the night I go.

He whistles for the dog. The dog barks.

Walkies!

Exit DICK. *Mad barking from the dog.*

JENNY: Very much his dog.

GWEN: Yes. A drink?

JENNY: I'm not. The baby.

GWEN: Sorry. I forgot.

JENNY: If you want one.

GWEN: No. I just thought you might like one.

JENNY *yawns.*

Tired?

JENNY: I didn't sleep much. I knew it would be positive but until I saw the doctor.

GWEN: I know.

JENNY: I was trying to think things through. And the German measles. There was a moment when I wanted to ring you but it was the middle of the night.

GWEN: I wouldn't have minded.

JENNY: I thought you mightn't recognise my voice. That you'd think I was a hoax. Or that Dick would answer. I thought you wouldn't know me.

GWEN: It took me a second.

JENNY: The light was going.

GWEN: Yes. The bed won't take long to air. Your old bed in your old room.

JENNY: It doesn't look like my room any more. I was expecting everything to be the same. Wallpaper, furniture, my teddy and bunnies on the bed. Where did they go?

GWEN: Do you want them?

JENNY: The baby might like them.

GWEN: You want new things for a baby.

JENNY: Sometimes I wished I'd taken them. My teddy, at least.

GWEN: Where did you go that first night?

JENNY: I went.

GWEN: Where?

JENNY: Oxford.

GWEN: I'm sorry. I said to myself that if you came back I wouldn't ask any questions. I wouldn't pry. I'd be pleased to see you and it wouldn't matter. I've worried about you for twenty years. And not one phone call or postcard. As if I'd never been, Jenny. Those phone calls when no one spoke when I answered. Was any of those you?

JENNY: No.

GWEN: I once phoned someone just to hear his voice.

JENNY: No!

GWEN: We thought you'd gone to London.

JENNY: That's why I went to Oxford.

GWEN: Did you know we were looking for you?

JENNY: I knew you would. I changed my name for a while.

GWEN: Dick said you must have done. I thought you might go to your father.

JENNY: You'd have found me.

GWEN: You can imagine what it was like with him. The accusations of being a bad mother. What he said about Dick. He's dead. Did you know that?

JENNY: No.

GWEN: He got drunk one night and drove into a canal.

JENNY: I'm sorry.

GWEN: I couldn't tell you how many years ago. Six, seven. A sad man. I should have let him go in the first place after the war. Getting pregnant with you was a cheap trick to pull on him. I was desperate. I thought I'd die if he went back to the States. What time are you going in the morning?

JENNY: I'm not working. Whenever.

GWEN: I try to leave by eight-thirty. Gives me an hour to see to the post. I like to start the mornings with my desk clear. You don't have to go when I go. You could sleep in. Have breakfast in bed.

JENNY: I could see your office. We could have lunch.

GWEN: I never have lunch – no – that would be lovely. There's a Boots across the road. They do teddies and rattles and things.

JENNY: Not yet. Please not yet.

GWEN: No, of course. When you're sure you could let me know and I could send something.

JENNY: We could have a look tomorrow. I could choose what I wanted and then you'd know.

GWEN: Yes. You could stay the weekend if you wanted.

JENNY: There's someone I have to see.

GWEN: Eric?

JENNY: Yes. Usually he has his daughter but not this weekend.

GWEN: You could invite him down.

JENNY: He's always talking about weekends in the country. Rugged. Not my sort of thing at all.

GWEN: There'd be no problems. I wouldn't try and push you.

JENNY: Divorce must be a good money spinner for estate agents.

GWEN: Yes. Hard though sometimes. There was a couple I showed round a house when they were engaged. I sold it them as a lovenest and no doubt he carried her over the doorstep.

Enter DICK.

He went back there one night after it was put on the market. Chopped up the floors with an axe. I know it's not professional but my heart bled. Have you locked?

DICK: Yes.

JENNY: It's very quiet here after London.

GWEN: Yes.

JENNY: I've got double glazing but the noise still comes in, and of course in the summer with the windows open – (*She yawns.*)

GWEN: You should go to bed.

JENNY: Um.

GWEN: I've put a towel on your bed and a nightie.

JENNY: Thank you.

DICK: Do you want to be woken in the morning?

JENNY *shakes her head.*

Anything special for breakfast?

JENNY: Just tea not coffee. I'm not that fussy.

GWEN: I may not see you in the morning.

JENNY: Lunch?

GWEN: Yes.

JENNY: I'll find you. Goodnight.

GWEN: Sleep well.

JENNY: Thank you for the supper.

DICK: Goodnight Jenny.

JENNY *goes.*

GWEN: She went to Oxford.

DICK: When?

GWEN: The first night.

DICK: It's one of the places we thought.

GWEN: Was it?

DICK: Where didn't we think?

GWEN: You didn't go there.

DICK: I couldn't look everywhere.

Pause.

I spent a week at Paddington watching every train. Every person who got off. Every dubious man that approached girls who were uncertain where to go. If you wanted Oxford scouring you could have done it from here.

GWEN: What if I'd been out and she'd come home?

DICK: She had her own keys.

GWEN: I wanted to be there.

Pause.

DICK: She asked if there were any photos

left of her as a baby. I said I didn't know. Are there?

GWEN: Yes.

DICK: Oh.

GWEN: Did you think I'd thrown them away?

DICK: Yes.

GWEN: My own daughter?

DICK: I thought so.

GWEN: They're in the office. Photos, her baby teeth, cards she made me at school. Her teddy and the bunnies. She has a file. Locked. I didn't want to keep stumbling on them. Do you like her?

DICK: Difficult to say so quicky. You?

GWEN: I'm her mother. It needs time.

DICK: She might go as suddenly as she came Gwen.

GWEN: She's staying tomorrow. And perhaps the weekend. The longer she stays . . .

DICK: I have things to do tomorrow.

GWEN: She can look after herself. She's not a child.

DICK: Come to bed.

GWEN: I've got some work.

DICK: Please Gwen.

GWEN: She and I are having lunch tomorrow. I have to. Or I'll never catch myself up.

DICK: You'll kill yourself.

GWEN: There's a contract I must push through tomorrow. Go to bed. I won't be long.

DICK: Wake me.

GWEN: Perhaps.

Pause.

Go to bed.

She kisses him.

Go.

DICK *goes.*
    GWEN *finds the acorn in her pocket. She looks for something to grow the acorn in.*

GWEN *tries to suspend the acorn above water.*
She unthreads three needles from the tapestry.
She stabs them in the acorn so it will balance over the water.
Enter JENNY *wearing* GWEN's *nightdress.*

JENNY: You are sure about the German measles?

GWEN: Certain.

JENNY *goes.*

Scene Three

The wood.
Enter ERIC.

ERIC: Lottie would love it here.

He stamps on chestnuts to get them from their cases.

These are empty as well. The woods are dying out. Any luck?

JENNY (*off*): None.

ERIC: I promised Lottie we'd roast chestnuts together when I got back.

JENNY (*off*): Buy some.

ERIC: Not the same.

JENNY (*off*): She'll never know.

He hides.

ERIC: Chestnuts from the woods Jen. It was a promise.

Enter JENNY.

JENNY: Eric! Look don't. Please don't. With Lottie. Not me. I hate it. Eric?

He jumps on her.

Don't.

ERIC: Jen?

JENNY: You nearly scared the bloody life out of me.

ERIC: Nature red in tooth and claw.

JENNY: Don't!

ERIC: Sorry.

JENNY: They can see from the house.

ERIC: No one to see. Your mother's working, your father's shopping.

JENNY: I don't –

ERIC: Should I change my toothpaste or something?

JENNY: My mother's house.

ERIC: What do they think goes on between us?

JENNY: Not them. Me.

ERIC: Why?

JENNY: It doesn't feel – I can't. Could you at your parents?

ERIC: Depend on you, wouldn't it?

JENNY: Have you?

ERIC: With Linda of course. Let's not discuss Linda.

JENNY: Sorry.

ERIC: If we'd spent the weekend in London?

JENNY: Yes probably. A bottle of wine and we usually do.

ERIC: But you're not drinking at the moment.

JENNY: No.

ERIC: If you want me to go I'll go. I'll spend the weekend at Linda's playing snakes and ladders with Lottie.

JENNY: Don't go.

ERIC: What's happened?

JENNY: Nothing.

ERIC: There has to be something Jenny. You come back here after how long? Demand I come too, then you treat me like a stranger.

JENNY: It's not to do with you.

ERIC: You were up and out like someone had shouted fire on Thursday morning. You didn't even say goodbye.

JENNY: I tried not to wake you.

ERIC: That's not what I'm complaining about.

He stamps on chestnuts.
He discovers a ball and throws it to JENNY.

Catch.

She does.

JENNY: It must be Cleo's.

ERIC: Surely you should throw a dog sticks in a wood.

JENNY *throws the ball back.*

You don't think I could keep it. Something to take back for Lottie?

JENNY: I won't say anything.

He throws the ball back to her.

ERIC: This time last year Lottie couldn't catch. This year she can. Linda's taught her I suppose.

JENNY: I've caught.

ERIC: What?

JENNY: Caught. It's the expression the little girls that come down from the North use. Pregnant.

ERIC: Fuck.

JENNY: Exactly.

ERIC: You can't be.

JENNY: But I am.

Pause.

ERIC: I'll pay for the abortion of course.

JENNY: I don't want you to.

ERIC: We'll go Dutch then.

JENNY: I don't want any money.

ERIC: You might let me play some part.

JENNY: You'll be a father.

ERIC: What?

JENNY: Its father. Is that so very difficult to understand?

ERIC: You're having it?

JENNY: Is that so very unusual?

ERIC: But when we talked about – accidents.

JENNY: We were talking.

ERIC: It is an accident?

JENNY: My mother had me to keep my father. You think I'd make the same mistake?

ERIC: You don't have to make a mistake. You know that.

JENNY: I didn't think that offer was open at the moment.

ERIC: It's always open.

JENNY: Sometimes more than others though?

ERIC: It's open. I've said I'll marry you. I won't unsay it because of this. Only this time you ask.

JENNY: I'm not asking.

ERIC: You never will.

JENNY: No, probably not.

ERIC: But us? Your job? Everything, your age. You're nearly forty.

JENNY: Thirty-eight. That's why.

ERIC: A baby's hard work Jen. I've done it.

JENNY: I haven't.

ERIC: You haven't been to the moon.

JENNY: I haven't had the chance.

ERIC: It's not that I don't want you to have it.

JENNY: It's mine. In me. There. Mine.

ERIC: How long?

JENNY: About six weeks.

ERIC: This big Jen.

JENNY: Yes.

ERIC: Jenny it's nappies, broken nights, total responsibility.

JENNY: So.

ERIC: Nothing will be the same again. Never.

JENNY: It's hardly how I'd planned the rest of my life. It used to be that when I was a day late I assumed I was pregnant. This time I assumed it was the menopause come early. It's not. I am. The proper tests. The scrubbed out jar and urine sample at dawn. I have conceived.

ERIC: An egg and a sperm Jen. Hardly a miracle.

JENNY: Better news than chestnuts.

Pause.

ERIC: Better news than the chestnuts. I can't wait to tell Lottie.

JENNY: Not yet.

ERIC: But you're certain.

JENNY: Not that there'll be a child at the end of it.

ERIC: That's what Linda – what every woman thinks when she first gets pregnant.

JENNY: Lottie's got Rubella. Spotty Lottie. The list of what it can do to a foetus is pretty impressive, blind it, deafen it, maim it –

ERIC: Not Lottie's fault.

JENNY: I know.

ERIC: A child of ten to have that hung round her neck –

JENNY: A virus, not Lottie.

ERIC: Don't blame her.

JENNY: No –

ERIC: Any of those things she'd blame herself.

JENNY: What about me?

ERIC: You're a grown-up. You understand.

JENNY: That there are risks. Yes, yes I do. I got a full list of them on Thursday morning. No congratulations. No smiles and handshakes. When the doctor looked at her notes she was positively apologetic. The suit and the briefcase. I suppose I hardly looked the maternal role. She started on the fact that I was more likely to have twins and ended on the increased risks of mongolism. She asked me if I'd had German measles and I said I didn't know, but that I'd seen Lottie and she had it. The doctor told me to ask my mother.

ERIC: There had to be some reason –

JENNY: I don't like sleepless nights.

ERIC: You haven't started yet.

JENNY: My mother put me out of my misery. The list of my childhood ailments is quite comprehensive. It includes Rubella. I'm in the clear.

ERIC: For certain?

JENNY: So far so good. More snakes than ladders at my age. I'll have to have an amniocentesis. That shows up mongolism and spina bifida and a host of other disasters and the baby's sex. But not until the sixteenth week. After that it's decision time. If I don't get rid of the child I have to get rid of the flat. My stairs would be impossible with a pram.

ERIC: Live with me.

JENNY: I don't love you.

ERIC: You don't have to.

JENNY: I do.

ERIC: Then how can I be its father?

JENNY: You'll always be welcome.

ERIC: I already have a child for weekends.

JENNY: It doesn't have to be weekends.

ERIC: Two nights a week like playing squash? Like Lottie? Never seeing her learn just the results of what Linda taught her. I can't bear that again Jenny. I'd rather go now and know nothing more.

JENNY: Eric!

ERIC: I'd rather go now Jen.

Pause.

Please.

JENNY: I don't know.

ERIC: I'd rather be sent away Jen.

Pause.

JENNY: I need you.

ERIC: What for?

JENNY: I do.

When ERIC *turns to walk away he meets* DICK.

DICK: Great thing about the autumn, makes it difficult for people to get lost here. I could see you from the bathroom. Not much luck?

ERIC: No.

DICK: A bit late perhaps.

JENNY: I don't think so. The cases are still green.

DICK: They're all about this size. Not worth the effort.

JENNY: The way you stamp on them anything decent would be smashed.

ERIC: I haven't got gloves.

DICK: Shouldn't need to get your fingers pricked. They should burst of their own accord once they're ripe. Still better luck next year. You'll have to come down again. I usually pop down to the local for lunch. I thought you might care to come.

I'm a cider man myself but there's a lot of praise for the beer.

ERIC: Jenny?

JENNY: It sounds nice.

DICK: Their steak and kidney pudding is certainly to be recommended over mine.

ERIC: I'll take these off. Put some proper shoes on.

DICK: Probably be as well.

JENNY: Can you get my purse?

ERIC: Whole bag?

JENNY: Just my money.

DICK: My treat.

JENNY: A working woman Dick. I pay my own way.

DICK: We'll see. The door's on the latch. Just pull it behind you.

He goes.

I like him.

JENNY: Thank you.

DICK: The outdoor type?

JENNY: Yes.

DICK: A walker?

JENNY: When he has the time.

DICK: You're not.

JENNY: Never have been.

DICK: Your mother neither. A stroll through the woods at the end of the day, that's all. Perhaps he might care to come with me tomorrow. Weather permitting. Take Cleo up to the downs, give her her head off the lead.

JENNY: He'd probably like that.

DICK: Be nice for me. A companion. You wouldn't mind?

JENNY: As long as I don't have to go.

DICK: You should come with us. A lot of people enjoy it once they get going. Put roses in your cheeks.

JENNY: Am I pale?

DICK: Well – you had such good colour.

JENNY: Used to. Did Gwen tell you I was pregnant?

DICK: Should she have done?

JENNY: I am.

DICK: Really?

JENNY: Yes.

DICK: Congratulations.

JENNY: Only just –

DICK: But still. (*He moves towards her.*) You must be delighted. Congratulations!

JENNY: You know there's not going to be a wedding?

DICK: Hardly matters nowadays does it? You must be thrilled?

JENNY: Sort of. Yes.

DICK: A grandchild. Gwen's grandchild.

JENNY: And you.

DICK: Not my own flesh and blood.

JENNY: Dick –

DICK: Eric's baby?

JENNY: Yes.

DICK: He's got a daughter by his first wife already hasn't he?

JENNY: Her mother has custody.

DICK: Best thing. Mothers are the ones who are good at all that sort of thing. I can do food and washing but nappies and bottles would have foxed me. Gwenny!

Enter GWEN.

GWEN: Hello! – To what do we owe this? – We have guests. I wondered where you all were. The house all unlocked. Eric says you're off to the pub.

DICK: What about the office?

GWEN: The girls would have to cope if I was ill. Have you had a good morning Jenny?

JENNY: Thank you.

DICK: They had breakfast and washed it all up.

GWEN: Good.

ERIC *enters. He gives* JENNY *her purse.*

JENNY: Thank you.

DICK: All on me. Seeing it's a celebration. I believe you're to be congratulated?

ERIC: Oh – er – Jen not me.

JENNY: Eric.

DICK: Both of you.

ERIC: Thanks. The door's locked. You have got keys.

DICK: I have mine.

DICK starts to lead ERIC across the stage.

I was thinking of going up on the Downs tomorrow. Ten miles or so. Jenny says you might care to come.

They are out of ear shot.

GWEN: Now we all know.

JENNY: Yes, you didn't tell him.

GWEN: You asked me not to. A secret between us. Pillow talk's not all it's cracked up to be.

JENNY: No.

GWEN: I like Eric. I thought he'd be – one doesn't really think of the private lives of accountants. He's nice.

JENNY: Mother.

GWEN: That's all. Honestly Jenny. I've never imagined I'd see you radiant in white.

JENNY: Once upon a time?

GWEN: That's what everyone expected. White, flowers, churches, true love.

JENNY: Babies?

GWEN: Of course. I'm glad you've stayed.

DICK (*off*): Come on.

GWEN: We don't usually have lunch together on Saturdays. The day most people look at houses. A deciding day. No buying and selling. You can't get anything moving, banks, building societies, anything like that.

JENNY: I moved in on a Saturday.

GWEN: All the finances will have gone through on the Friday at the latest.

JENNY: It's funny to hear you being a business woman.

GWEN: Is it?

JENNY: Of course.

GWEN: I'm sorry.

JENNY: Your work.

GWEN: More like life sometimes.

DICK *comes back.*

Yes, yes we're coming. I'll just shut the gate!

ERIC: It'll be closing time.

JENNY: Rounding us up?

DICK: It gets very full. We won't get a table for four.

ERIC: Race you Jenny. First one there buys the drinks!

JENNY: A game we play with his daughter. He always likes to win. He buys us ice creams.

ERIC: Come on.

JENNY runs.

DICK: Should she run like that?

GWEN: Now you know why she's come back.

DICK: Yes.

GWEN: Another thing we were wrong about.

DICK: Nicer than a grandchild suddenly turning up fully grown. A baby.

GWEN: I'm not keen on small babies.

DICK: Jenny.

GWEN: Not even Jenny. Not at the very beginning. Moments of course when my heart melted. Times when she was quite defenceless. But other moments when I loathed her. I had a black angora cardigan. Very precious after the war. She was sick on it. Ruined it.

DICK: A silly thing to wear with a little baby.

GWEN: She was pretty and cooed over. I wanted to feel special. I never dared afford another.

DICK: You could now.

GWEN: They have to go to the dry cleaners.

DICK: We can afford dry cleaners.

GWEN: Not if I went bankrupt tomorrow.

DICK: Are you likely to?

GWEN: Of course not. But I couldn't bear to have one and not afford to have it cleaned. Jenny has all that to find out.

They stop.

I held a pillow over her face once. Not very hard, not very tight – not even very long. She wouldn't even have whimpered.

DICK: Why didn't you?

GWEN: I didn't.

DICK: What stopped you?

GWEN: The effort I'd put in. You want to hang on.

Pause.

We're not taking Cleo?

DICK: She'd only have to stay outside.

GWEN: Seems mean to leave her on her own.

They go.

Scene Four

The Wood.
After lunch. ERIC *and* JENNY. ERIC *has bought a pound of chestnuts for Lottie.*

ERIC: Far too many. You don't mind if I go with him tomorrow?

JENNY: Rather you than me that's all.

ERIC: I like him.

JENNY: I meant the walking.

ERIC: He's hardly your description of him.

JENNY: People change. He's mellowed. And my mother?

ERIC: Mothers are mothers.

He looks in the bag.

Far too many.

JENNY: Half of them are probably bad.

ERIC: Do you think so?

JENNY: The risk you take.

They have crossed the stage.

Scene Five

The house.
   ERIC *and* DICK *are making a swiss roll for* GWEN's *birthday.*

JENNY *is cracking eggs into a bowl.*
   DICK *is lining a swiss roll tin with greaseproof paper.*

JENNY: Oh God.

ERIC: It doesn't mean it's fertilized.

JENNY: It turns my stomach.

DICK: Why don't you go next door? The fire's lit.

JENNY: I think I might.

She stops.

You have remembered to put the oven on?

ERIC: Yes.

She goes.

DICK: Gwen always says that. Is the oven on? The obvious thing to do is to put that at the beginning of the recipe but they never do.

ERIC: I whisk this lot together over hot water?

DICK *consults the recipe.*

DICK: Yes.

ERIC *does so.*

And four ounces of plain flour.

DICK *weighs it.*

Ought to be sieved I suppose. Don't want any disasters.

ERIC: There aren't going to be any.

DICK (*sifting flour*): I can't see how it's going to rise without baking powder or something.

ERIC: The eggs.

Enter JENNY.

JENNY: Bowl.

She takes the washing up bowl.

Thank you.

She goes.

ERIC: Poor Jen.

DICK: The doctor recommended Gwen had champagne. I pointed out we couldn't afford it, he said lemonade would do just as well.

ERIC (*mixing on the cooker*): Sorry?

DICK: For morning sickness. He told Gwen to have champagne. Didn't realise it went on for so long, I suppose, because she lost the baby.

ERIC: I'm sorry.

DICK: Yes.

ERIC: Your baby?

DICK: Yes. Mine –

ERIC: Sorry.

DICK: Long time ago –

Pause.

ERIC: Next?

DICK: Remove from heat. Fold in flour and water with metal spoon.

ERIC: Metal spoon?

DICK: In the drawer.

ERIC *finds it.*

Careful, you'll burn it.

ERIC *takes the pan off the heat.*

ERIC: Sorry.

ERIC *begins to stir in the flour.*

DICK: Touch and go from the first. I never thought Gwen's heart was really in it. She had this notion. She ought to give me a child. She had Jenny. And Jenny was almost grown-up. Shaped before I met her. Spoilt. What she wanted she got. Gwen stinted herself to give Jenny things. Still you can see why it happened, just her and Gwen together.

ERIC: I sometimes think Linda's too strict with Lottie. A lot of mustn'ts, not allowed. You will make sure she cleans her teeth whenever she's eaten.

ERIC *tastes.* DICK *looks at him.*

Cook's prerogative.

DICK: I did want a child. I never pressed her but she felt she owed it me. When Jenny went, her womb let go –

ERIC *has begun to scrape the mixture into the tin.*

Bleeding and bleeding and bleeding. Everything in it. No torrent just an oozing, like the sap from a tree. Day after day. A slipping away. In clots. It could have been any of them. She said there was

no pain, nothing, that it was Jenny she was crying for. Soak the sheets she said. First cold water and then boiling. I buried them in the wood, it might at least have done some good. I didn't want to see the froth on the top of the pan like boiling bones. They scraped Gwen out, though what there was to scrape. No question of children after that.

He picks up the tin.

In?

ERIC: Might as well.

DICK *puts the cake in the oven.*

DICK: How long?

ERIC: Seven to nine minutes.

DICK *sets the timer.*

Want to scrape?

DICK: Seems a shame to waste it.

ERIC: Yes.

They sit down to scrape the bowl.

This is the bit Lottie likes best.

DICK: My mother always used to leave some on the spoon. Not very much but she never pushed it off with her finger. My treat.

ERIC: Lottie's treat too. With me.

DICK: Must be nice watching her grow up.

ERIC: Yes.

DICK: You should bring her down. Fresh air. The woods to run in.

ERIC: Lottie'd love that.

DICK: Bring her.

ERIC: Perhaps.

DICK: Better wash all this up before Gwen gets back.

ERIC: What about candles?

DICK: Too old for candles.

ERIC: Special birthday. She ought to have them.

DICK: You can't put candles on a swiss roll.

ERIC: You've got some?

DICK: For power cuts. In the drawer. Gwen doesn't like the dark.

ERIC *gets out the candles.*

Not birthday candles.

ERIC: Better than nothing.

DICK: She'll think we're making a fuss of her.

ERIC: Aren't we? Lottie's like the queen. She has two birthdays, one with me and one with her mother. Cake and candles at each.

DICK: Never made Gwen a cake before. We usually go out for dinner.

ERIC: No point going out for dinner with Jenny in her condition.

DICK: No.

ERIC: A notch for every decade.

Enter JENNY.

JENNY: All over?

ERIC: Yes. A notch for every decade. Ten, twenty, thirty, forty, fifty, sixty. Is she going to retire?

DICK: She says she won't. No one to take over.

ERIC: She could sell.

DICK: Not yet she says.

JENNY: She'll have to eventually.

DICK: Try telling her that.

JENNY: She might as well do it while she can still spend the money.

DICK: My point entirely.

ERIC: She ought to get a partner. Someone who could take over from her gradually.

JENNY: The ideal sort of job to do part-time I'd have thought. You have set the timer.

ERIC: Yes.

JENNY: Sometimes people forget.

DICK: Don't worry. There we are, all ship-shape. Gwen'll have no idea of what we've been cooking up. I think I'll just take Cleo down to the stream. You coming?

JENNY: Go if you want. I can be left.

ERIC: I'll look after the cake.

DICK: Right.

DICK goes.

ERIC: You okay?

JENNY: It was just that egg. Silly really. Was Linda like this?

ERIC: Not as bad as you've been.

JENNY: Do you think I'm making a fuss?

ERIC: My experience is limited.

JENNY: Mother said she was sick but an easy labour. I seem to be on course for a pretty similar experience to hers.

ERIC: You know she had a miscarriage?

JENNY: Linda?

ERIC: Gwen.

JENNY: No.

ERIC: She did Jenny.

JENNY: I don't want to hear.

Pause.

They say you have contractions when you miscarry. Do you think that's true?

ERIC: I don't know.

JENNY: When?

ERIC: When you left. You didn't know?

JENNY: I had no idea. It's my fault I suppose?

ERIC: Dick didn't say that.

JENNY: Is that what they think? There could have been a hundred reasons. She must have been older than me, there could have been all sorts of things wrong. Better that than a – don't you think?

ERIC: She didn't tell you?

JENNY: I didn't ask. She knew I was pregnant. She stood there and she looked at me and she knew I was. She could tell . . . Twenty years.

ERIC: Intuition. Linda had that about Lottie. When Lottie was a baby she could tell what the cries meant. If it was nappy or food or colic.

JENNY: Do you think I will?

ERIC: Depends doesn't it.

JENNY: It could all be so perfect. But it won't be will it? When they put that needle in through my navel.

ERIC: It could be Jenny.

JENNY: Don't say it. You know how things go wrong if you say them. Did Dick tell you?

ERIC: Yes.

JENNY: You get on very well with them.

ERIC: Nice people.

JENNY: Really?

ERIC: Really.

JENNY: I find it hard to tell. Whether they're being nice to me or whether they aren't.

ERIC: Twenty years. You can't expect it to sort itself out in a few visits. Not even friends in that time.

JENNY: They're parents, not friends.

ERIC: It's a lovely place to live.

JENNY: Could you live here. In the country I mean?

ERIC: Love to if it wasn't for work and Lottie.

JENNY: It's a lovely place for children. I used to play such games in the woods. And so safe. It's safe here. You could have a child here and not be worried about it every minute.

ERIC: Trees to fall from. Streams to drown in.

JENNY: It's a different sort of danger.

ERIC: You thinking of moving here?

JENNY: Not for myself but for the baby.

ERIC: Don't talk about it you said.

JENNY: It's very hard to have no plans at all. No thought. I can't have it inside me and not in my head.

ERIC: It's a dream, Jenny. What would you do here? What is there?

JENNY: But if I was here with a baby would you come?

ERIC: On what conditions?

JENNY: Like we are now. You could commute from Didcot.

ERIC: I'm not the commuting sort. Neither are you a housewife. And anyway Lottie's in London.

JENNY: Do you have to be where Lottie is?

ERIC: What do you want?

JENNY: I don't believe in happy endings.

The buzzer on the oven goes.

ERIC: Could you put a damp tea towel under there please.

She does so. ERIC *turns the swiss roll out.*

JENNY: Perfect.

ERIC: It isn't rolled yet.

Scene Six

The wood.
  Christmas Eve. Enter JENNY *in nightdress.*

JENNY: Child? Child? Can you hear me? Your mother. Me. Are you there? Child? Please. Move. Quicken. Just once. Something. It's Christmas. Do you know that? Christmas Eve. After midnight so Christmas really. Do you know when it's light or night? Can you tell when I'm asleep? If I'm happy? Or I'm sad? Do you know? Anything. Please. Your mother. Child.

She waits.
  Enter ERIC.

Who's there?

ERIC: Father Christmas.

JENNY: Have you got your reindeer?

ERIC: Having a rest.

JENNY: Oh.

ERIC: Have you hung your stockings up, little girl?

JENNY: I'm too old for stockings.

ERIC: You could still make an old man very happy.

Pause.

Come in. You'll get cold.

JENNY: Can't sleep.

ERIC: Not likely to sleep much out here.

JENNY: I'm so frightened.

He holds her.

ERIC: Don't be.

JENNY: I am.

They stand in the wood.
  They are caught in a car headlight.
  They hide their eyes.
  The light goes.

They're back from church.

ERIC: Yes.

JENNY: Happy Christmas.

ERIC: Happy Christmas.

JENNY: I wonder what tomorrow will be like? What the rituals are?

ERIC: The same as when you left presumably.

JENNY: Think so?

ERIC: Christmases tend to be.

JENNY: Like being a child again.

ERIC: I wonder what Lottie's doing.

JENNY: Be asleep by now.

ERIC: Yes.

JENNY: She have a stocking?

ERIC: Pillowcases. In Linda's family they have pillowcases.

JENNY: Oh.

ERIC: And beef for Christmas dinner. My turn for Lottie next year.

JENNY: What will you do?

ERIC: Depends on Lottie.

JENNY: And me?

ERIC: Goes without saying.

JENNY: Do you think it knew when the needle went in?

ERIC: They're supposed to be able to hear music. Some people play them Mozart.

JENNY: If there's any blood I have to ring the hospital immediately. One of the things the amniocentesis can do. There are risks and risks and risks. It would be easier not to have the chance in the first place.

ERIC: There won't be any bleeding. It'll be okay. The results will all be positive. All systems go.

JENNY: No.

ERIC: Come in.

JENNY: I can't sleep.

ERIC: Tell you a story. Lottie's favourite. Once upon a time there was a king's daughter who lived in a palace on the top of a hill. And because she was a king's daughter she was a princess. One day the princess said to the king I want to find a handsome prince to marry –

He has walked her off stage.
  Enter GWEN.
  She whistles for Cleo.
  She sings to herself.

GWEN: The angel Gabriel from heaven came
His wings as drifted snow
His eyes as flame
All hail said he
Thou lowly maiden Mary
Most highly favoured lady
Gloria.

She has gone.

ACT TWO

Scene One

GWEN's *office.*
GWEN *is working.* Enter JENNY.

GWEN: Hello.

JENNY: I saw her. All her bones like a feather. Like a fossil in a rock. I had to come down and tell you.

GWEN: And everything's all right?

JENNY: Perfect. Her heart beats.

GWEN: I'm glad.

JENNY: A little girl. They asked if I wanted to know that. I wanted to know everything. She's even got a name. I had thought Anna but suddenly Jessica just came into my head. A name I'd never thought of before. Jessica.

GWEN: I thought of calling you Anna. Ann. After your grandmother. But your father thought differently. He registered your birth. Made you a Jennifer. Shouldn't you ask Eric?

JENNY: My daughter. Jessica.

GWEN: How can you name a child before it's born?

JENNY: I've seen her. My baby, Jessica.

GWEN *goes to the filing cabinet. She unlocks it. From a drawer she takes* JENNY's *teddy etc.*

GWEN: I didn't want to keep stumbling across them. I didn't want Dick to know how I longed.

There is a long moment. JENNY *picks up the teddy.*

Twenty years. Twenty Christmases and twenty birthdays. Not one letter. Not one phone call. Not one postcard. You might at least have bestowed hate on me. You might have had the grace to hurt me face to face.

JENNY: It wasn't you. It was Dick.

GWEN: Then me through Dick. We could have sorted something out. We could have talked about it.

JENNY: You wouldn't have talked.

GWEN: But to run away. I told myself an hour, a day, a week, a month, a year. Then she'll be back. When we were burgled I didn't let Dick change the lock. Because you had a key.

JENNY: I threw it in the river at Oxford. The day I changed my name.

Pause.

GWEN: What did you call yourself?

JENNY: Katherine.

GWEN: Katherine

JENNY: Katherine. With a K.

GWEN: Why?

JENNY: It could be Kate, Kath, Kathy, any number of things.

GWEN: Which did you prefer?

JENNY: There are still people who call me Kate.

GWEN: From a long time ago?

JENNY: Quite a long time. There was someone who called me Kitty I liked that.

GWEN: Someone you were fond of?

JENNY: More than that.

GWEN: It didn't work?

JENNY: He went away. His job. It was important for him.

GWEN: He didn't ask you to go with him?

JENNY: He asked.

GWEN: You should have gone.

JENNY: I'd just bought my own flat. How could I? What would I have done on my own abroad if anything went wrong? He never wrote. Different to Eric. A million miles apart.

GWEN: Don't go. Not completely. Not again. I couldn't bear it.

JENNY: The thing I won't be able to do with a child is travel. I know there'll be other satisfactions of course. But that's been the joy of the job I do. Being able to come and go.

GWEN: You can't come and go in this job. I don't even take holidays.

JENNY: Wouldn't you like to? You and Dick? Go somewhere nice together? Somewhere warm?

GWEN: I don't want to come and go.

JENNY: Not at all?

GWEN: No, I have no feelings of discontent. Oh, that a deal would happen faster, that a structural survey was better. Not for myself.

JENNY: But you should do.

GWEN: Why?

JENNY: Do you have no ambition?

GWEN: Is that so very hard to understand?

JENNY: Yes.

GWEN: For years what I wanted was for you to come back. You've come . . . There's nothing now.

JENNY: Jessica?

Pause.

She's real now mother. A real child.

She looks at the teddy.

Was he always like this – his nose squashed?

GWEN: You loved him too much.

JENNY: Heaven knows why. Revolting old thing. Fancy saving him all this time.

She throws the teddy away.

You were right. You want new things for a baby. The very best of everything.

Enter DICK.

DICK: Well?

JENNY: Perfect.

DICK: We have lift off?

JENNY: Yes. A little girl.

GWEN *rescues the teddy.*

DICK: A girl.

JENNY: She's even got a name.

DICK: What a perfect start to the New Year.

JENNY: I saw her. Like a fossil in a rock. All her bones like a feather.

GWEN: Her name's Jessica.

DICK *sees the teddy in* GWEN's *arms. Pause.*

Have you taken Cleo out today?

DICK: I'll give her a proper run tomorrow. They're predicting a thaw.

GWEN: She should go out today.

DICK: She gets balls of ice in her fur. The floor will have to be mopped.

GWEN: I'll do it when I get back.

DICK: Eric must be pleased.

JENNY: I expect so. He'll be able to tell Lottie.

DICK: She'll be thrilled. A little sister.

JENNY: Yes.

DICK: We'll have to see about cots and things for when you come and stay.

GWEN: She'll have one of those carry cot ones. Won't you? That you can bring with you.

JENNY: I hadn't thought.

DICK: I'll cook something special. A celebration. Do you think you should get Eric to come down?

JENNY: He'd only have to go straight back and the roads are lethal. Especially in the dark.

GWEN: There are some duck portions in the freezer that need eating. If you take them out as soon as you get back they'll thaw for tonight.

DICK: Good.

Pause.

I should get back then. I'll see you both later.

JENNY: If I want to come back earlier will you be in?

DICK: If I've not taken Cleo out. We ought to give you keys. Then you can come and go as you please.

GWEN: She can always borrow mine.

JENNY: Be nice to have my own.

DICK: I'll get you one cut on my way home.

JENNY: You're an angel. Thanks.

DICK: It's a pleasure. And I'm delighted for you.

Exit DICK.

JENNY: I've bought some fabric. I thought you could make her dresses like you made me.

JENNY *gets the fabric out.*
  GWEN *fingers it. It is sensual for her.*

GWEN: Tana lawn. You had gingham.

JENNY: And this pattern.

GWEN: I can afford to buy things for my grandchild.

JENNY: Not the same thing.

GWEN: By the time you've cut out, pinned, tacked and sewn. Time is money.

JENNY: You could teach me.

GWEN: If I had time –

JENNY: If I helped you out here whenever I could. You could show me what to do. I'm used to buying and selling. Striking a hard bargain.

GWEN: Help me here?

JENNY: I'm a much better typist than you.

GWEN: You have a job.

JENNY: They have to give me maternity leave. I'll hate sitting around with time on my hands.

GWEN: You don't have time on your hands with a baby.

JENNY: When they're asleep. If I have a carry cot I'll be able to bring her with me. I could get on with things and still be there whenever she needed me. And you'll help won't you mother. Your grand-daughter.

GWEN: You should ring Eric. Tell him the good news.

JENNY: I wanted you to know first.

GWEN: The phone's there.

JENNY: I'll wait.

GWEN: I can go outside. You can be private.

JENNY: It can wait.

GWEN: Doesn't being certain make a difference?

JENNY: Why should it?

GWEN: A child'll be hard on your own Jenny. Hard.

Pause.

And lonely. So lonely you wouldn't believe it.

JENNY: I don't love him.

GWEN: You're fond of each other.

JENNY: Fond!

GWEN: I married Dick because I was fond of him. It wasn't anything like it was with your father.

JENNY: Not at the beginning though. Not in the very beginning?

GWEN: You were an onlooker.

JENNY: You were obsessed by him.

GWEN: Never.

JENNY: You were.

GWEN: Never Jenny.

JENNY: Cuddles, giggles, pulling your skirt down on the sofa.

GWEN: No.

JENNY: Dick this, Dick that. Always. He likes eggs for his breakfast. We must all have eggs.

GWEN: Cooking one breakfast instead of three.

JENNY: But his choice.

GWEN: He was paying the grocery bills.

JENNY: You married him for that?

GWEN: No.

JENNY: Then what?

GWEN: I was on my own.

JENNY: You had me.

GWEN: I was lonely. I don't mean to sound harsh but you were hardly a companion. He wanted me. You no longer had any need of me. Not really Jenny. Not a need I'd passed on everything I could.

JENNY: I need you now.

GWEN: You have Eric.

JENNY: Fond was the word.

GWEN: There's no room for great passion with a baby, Jenny. You don't have the energy. The nights are broken.

JENNY: I'll have Jessica.

GWEN: She won't be able to hold you when you feel like weeping.

JENNY: Then I won't weep.

GWEN: Can you be that strong?

JENNY: If I set my mind to it.

Pause.

GWEN: You frighten me.

JENNY: My own mother.

GWEN: Yes.

JENNY: Why don't you have a look at the pattern while I finish this.

Scene Two

Winter.
> *Early morning in the wood.*
> ERIC *crosses the stage. He is going back to London.*

JENNY (*off*): Eric. Darling.

> *He stops. Enter* JENNY *for the first time very visibly pregnant.*

> Please. I feel so ugly. I'm supposed to be radiant and I feel so ugly.

ERIC: I have to go.

JENNY: Ring.

ERIC: No.

JENNY: Am I so very hideous.

ERIC: No.

JENNY: Then stay.

ERIC: I promised Lottie.

JENNY: Can't Linda take her?

ERIC: Linda can't swim.

JENNY: Why not?

ERIC: She never learnt. I have to take Lottie.

JENNY: I could ring her. Lottie would understand.

ERIC: Jenny, Lottie doesn't understand. That is why I have to go.

JENNY: I feel so ugly.

ERIC: I'm sorry.

> *Pause.*

> I can't not go. I gave my word.

JENNY: Please.

ERIC: You sound like Lottie.

JENNY: Please.

ERIC: No.

JENNY: Just today.

ERIC: Today is the day we go swimming together. Lottie and me. Then we have a hamburger and she has a strawberry milkshake. Then we go to a film or the zoo or something fun. And she has an ice cream. Strawberry. And we do her homework and she stays the night with me.

JENNY: You could explain.

ERIC: I can't.

JENNY: It's very simple.

ERIC: She doesn't understand.

JENNY: She has sex education.

ERIC: The human biology of it. Yes. Match A to B and do C. She feels she's being left out. That I won't have enough time for her. That it'll be you and I and a baby –

JENNY: Jessica.

ERIC: She isn't born.

JENNY: She will be.

ERIC: That it'll be you and me and whatever you want to call it – her. And that Lottie will be left out.

JENNY: She won't be left out.

ERIC: She feels she will.

JENNY: That's ridiculous.

ERIC: Is it?

JENNY: Lottie's half-sister.

ERIC: Jenny I feel left out. And if I feel left out where does that leave her?

JENNY: I'm asking you to stay.

ERIC: Why?

JENNY: You know why.

ERIC: *Why?*

JENNY: I want you to make love to me.

ERIC: A fuck because you feel so ugly.

JENNY: Yes. I want you.

> *Pause.*

> I need you.

ERIC: It's not that I don't want you. I love you. I have to go.

> *Pause.*

I love Lottie you see.

JENNY: You love her most?

ERIC: My daughter.

JENNY: Your daughter here.

ERIC: I can't understand that.

JENNY: Didn't you with Lottie?

ERIC: Not till I saw her born. No. I used to lie with my head on Linda's belly and feel her kicking. Like a kitten in a sack.

GWEN *whistles for Cleo off stage.*

Gwen's up.

JENNY: Even I'm getting used to getting up early when I'm here.

ERIC: Morning.

Enter GWEN.

GWEN: Did you let Cleo out?

JENNY: Oh God, I left the door. I'm sorry.

GWEN: Why don't you think sometimes.

JENNY: I'm sorry.

GWEN: You have a key. You can let yourself out, you can let yourself in.

JENNY: I'm sorry.

ERIC: She won't have gone far will she.

GWEN: How should I know?

Enter DICK.

Cleo's done a bolt.

JENNY: I'm sorry.

GWEN: It's so irresponsible Jenny. Two seconds thought.

DICK: She's said she's sorry.

GWEN: There are early lambs you know that?

DICK: Cleo doesn't chase sheep.

GWEN: There's always the first time. They're allowed to shoot on sight. You know that?

JENNY: I'm sorry.

GWEN: Shoot to kill. Not to maim or warn off but to kill.

JENNY: I've said I'm sorry.

GWEN: The call of the wild. How's she supposed to resist?

DICK: Gwen this is silly.

GWEN: Your dog too.

DICK: She won't have gone far.

GWEN: She's out of ear shot. I've called her.

DICK: She comes much better on the whistle.

DICK *whistles.*

JENNY: I'm sorry.

DICK: You weren't to know.

GWEN: Don't treat her as if she's a child. I'd told her.

JENNY: I didn't realise.

DICK: Everybody round here knows her. No one will shoot her.

ERIC: More likely to get hit by a car.

JENNY: Oh shut up!

DICK: This happens time and time again when we're out walking. I walk on. Let her have her sniff of rabbit or whatever and when she's had a taste of freedom she comes back. Just when you don't expect it: there she is.

JENNY: Cleo! Cleo!

DICK: She comes much better on the whistle.

JENNY *attempts to whistle – it is hopeless.* DICK *whistles expertly. They wait.*

JENNY: Oh what's the point in standing here? Let's go and look for her.

ERIC: Which way is she likely to go?

GWEN: Depends on the temptation.

DICK: I'll go up to the farm.

JENNY: I'll come with you. Dick.

GWEN: Thank God she's not on heat. That's all we need a bitch in whelp.

They go. GWEN *and* ERIC *remain.*

ERIC: I'm sorry.

GWEN: Not your fault.

ERIC: In a way. She wanted to say good-bye to me. I thought she was asleep.

GWEN: Your weekend for Lottie?

ERIC: Um.

GWEN: I'd like to meet her.

ERIC: Perhaps one day.

GWEN: You'd be very welcome to bring her here.

ERIC: Thank you. It's kind of you.

GWEN: I mean it.

ERIC: Things are very difficult at the moment. Jealousy I think. Lottie won't have anything to do with me. I'm supposed to take her swimming. The past couple of times he's refused to come with me. I don't like to force the issue.

GWEN: Sounds like Jenny and Dick. She wouldn't speak to him. She developed a system of grunts that could mean either yes or no. I –
    Cleo! Cleo!
    We don't have many chances to talk you and I.

ERIC: No.

GWEN: It's only natural that I should worry about her.

ERIC: Yes.

GWEN: You have behaved very decently. I do think that. But what will happen.

ERIC: I don't know.

GWEN: Do you love her?

ERIC: I – I'm –

GWEN: I'm finding it very difficult. I do want to. Her mother. I should. But – there are times I don't know what to say. Twenty years of silence. Her past. I don't belong to it. It makes questions between us. Does she talk about me?

ERIC: Of course.

GWEN: Not now. When you first knew her? What did she say about me then? Was I castigated?

ERIC: She's never been a rememberer.

GWEN: She must have said things. You must have asked.

ERIC: She didn't talk about you.

GWEN: Nothing?

ERIC: Nothing. I'm sorry.

GWEN: Not even that she hated me?

ERIC: Nothing.

GWEN: You do love her, don't you?

ERIC: Yes.

GWEN: Does she know?

ERIC: Yes.

GWEN: I suppose you blame me.

ERIC: No.

GWEN: You must do sometimes.

ERIC: I just think one day she'll change.

GWEN: Or you might.

ERIC: We've broken up three or four times. It's always me who comes back.

GWEN: Why?

ERIC: I do.

Pause.

GWEN: I am trying Eric. I am trying. I've started to say to myself, perhaps when Jessica is born. Through Jessica. She'll have to think with a baby. Doesn't she realise that? Her life won't be her own ever again. She's made no preparations at all so far as I can see.

ERIC: She's put her flat on the market. Didn't you know?

GWEN: No. She's going to live with you?

ERIC: I have asked her Gwen. The answer's always no.

Pause.

    Isn't she coming here?

GWEN: Here?

ERIC: I thought that was the plan.

GWEN: She can't come here.

ERIC: You'll have to ask her.

GWEN: She can stay – you can both stay as often as you like of course. Did Dick ask her? Did he say she could.

ERIC: I don't want her to come here. It would make things impossible. Lottie is in London. I have to be where Lottie is. If Jenny comes here then it has to be over between us. It has to be.

GWEN: But she's coming?

ERIC: That's what she says. I have to go, Gwen.

He kisses GWEN.

GWEN: You'll look for Cleo?

ERIC: Of course.

GWEN: Are you coming back?

ERIC: Only one car. I'll come back for her tomorrow.

GWEN: I could take her to the station.

ERIC: I'll come.

He goes.
   GWEN *whistles for Cleo.*

Scene Three

The wood.
   A bit later. GWEN *is whistling for Cleo.*

DICK: Gwen, come and have breakfast. She'll be back when she's ready.

GWEN: It's not as if I haven't told Jenny.

DICK: You've said your piece for today.

GWEN: Well really.

DICK: Come and have breakfast.

GWEN: I don't want any.

DICK: Jenny's cooked it.

GWEN: No thank you.

DICK: You know you reduced her to tears.

GWEN: Don't be silly.

DICK: You did.

GWEN: I didn't mean to.

DICK: She's in a highly emotional state Gwen.

GWEN: I do know. I have been through pregnancy.

Enter JENNY.

JENNY: Your eggs'll be hard.

DICK: Right.

   DICK *goes into the house.*

JENNY: She moved.

GWEN: He says I made you cry?

JENNY: A kick. A real kick.

GWEN: Did I?

   Pause.

JENNY: I wish Eric hadn't gone. Am I coming into the office?

GWEN: Up to you.

JENNY: Do you need me?

GWEN: You know what Saturday mornings are like. We've got eleven accompanied viewings on the books at the moment.

JENNY: I'll do those shall I?

GWEN: It would help.

JENNY: Fine.

GWEN: Why are you so willing?

JENNY: Helping out.

GWEN: Why?

JENNY: You need help.

GWEN: Only because it's offered.

JENNY: So let me help.

GWEN: Do you want something?

JENNY: No.

GWEN: You're here every weekend.

JENNY: I've missed you.

GWEN: You could have come before.

JENNY: I'd left it too long. I needed an excuse.

GWEN: Because you wanted something.

JENNY: A few questions.

GWEN: You could have gone once they'd been answered.

JENNY: I didn't want to.

GWEN: Do you like it here with us? Two old people.

JENNY: It's home.

GWEN: Is it?

JENNY: I was brought up here. The place I've always remembered. I had my first kiss here. My first true kiss. It has memories for me.

GWEN: The cottage where I was born's five miles away. I didn't go there.

JENNY: I thought you were glad to grow up. Get away.

GWEN: Weren't you?

JENNY: It's quite safe here. Safe. I sleep at night.

GWEN: I hear your're selling your flat.

JENNY: Yes.

GWEN: Oh.

JENNY: A second floor flat without a lift will be impossible with a pram.

GWEN: Yes.

JENNY: I'm hoping to get around fifty thousand – of course there's my mortgage but – selling myself.

GWEN: I see.

JENNY: I'll do it mother, I will.

GWEN: Yes, you will.

JENNY: Of course you'll be the first person I'll come to if there are any problems. But aren't you proud of me? How much you've taught me? I wouldn't have had the first idea of what to do without you. We do work well together, don't we?

GWEN: I do loathe typing.

JENNY: Perhaps you should employ me as your secretary.

GWEN: I thought you'd done all that?

JENNY: Yes. I couldn't do it again. Not even for you. I'm used to being top dog now. There'll be money from the flat. I could put that into the agency. Twenty thousand, that would pay for more secretarial help. A duplicator, bigger premises. You'd be able to expand.

GWEN: I'm already run off my feet.

JENNY: I'd help. Together we could be so much bigger.

GWEN: Buy me?

JENNY: No. Put capital in. Favell and daughter on the boards. You don't see that do you? It would be good publicity. A little gimmick, the papers would pick up on it.

GWEN: Favell and mother. More interesting still.

JENNY: You see so many possibilities. And with the profits we could open another branch, a chain.

GWEN: I haven't said yes.

JENNY: It's a wonderful idea.

GWEN: Your idea.

JENNY: We'll be able to take turns with Jessica. Share her. All the cuddles you could want.

GWEN: And dirty nappies and broken nights?

JENNY: She's not going to be that sort of baby.

GWEN: All babies shit and puke. It's the one factor they have in common.

DICK (*off, shouting*): More toast going in now.

JENNY: I must eat before I go. You ought to have something.

GWEN: Not hungry.

JENNY: That's silly.

Pause.

I must have something. All those accompanieds. I'll wear my support tights.

GWEN: Do they help?

JENNY: Supposed to.

Enter DICK.

DICK: The food is going to be ruined.

JENNY: She doesn't want anything.

DICK: It's Cleo. You can always get another dog.

JENNY: I'll buy you one mother. The best. One with a pedigree.

DICK: You'll be late for work.

JENNY: I can't seem to start the day on an empty stomach.

She goes in.

GWEN: Did you invite her here. Tell her she could live here?

DICK: Plenty of space.

GWEN: It isn't that. Don't you see? I have tried Dick. I have tried.

DICK: I said it would take time.

GWEN: The more time there is the more gaps. I don't want her to live here. Please make her go. I don't want her here.

DICK: Your own daughter.

GWEN: Not mine. Someone else's. Not mine.

DICK: We get on swimmingly.

GWEN: You get on. I work my way from one day to another. Get rid of her.

DICK: How?

GWEN: It doesn't matter.

DICK: Play the heavy stepfather?

GWEN: If that's what you have to do.

DICK: No.

GWEN: Please. For me. Please.

DICK: I like her. I'm looking forward to there being a baby in the house.

GWEN: You know nothing about it.

DICK: I fetched her from that party for you. And wished a thousand times I never had.

GWEN: One o'clock in the morning I was worried sick.

DICK: Your daughter. You could have got her.

GWEN: I was pregnant.

DICK: That didn't stop Jenny coming here from London. I've never held a baby. All my life. Never.

GWEN: You'll get enough practice with Jenny's. Well who else do you think is going to look after it? That's why she's come.

Enter JENNY with bit of toast.

JENNY: Mother, you'll be late. Shall I keep your coffee?

GWEN: I'll have one in the office.

JENNY: What do you think about getting a proper coffee machine for the office? Be so much nicer for people than instant. I'll see you in a minute.

She goes to the car.

DICK: You see. She's a great help.

GWEN: Watching me. Criticising me because I give people instant coffee.

DICK: They do things differently in London.

GWEN: Then let her stay there. She's worming herself in Dick. Can't you see that?

DICK: But you wanted her?

GWEN: Not like this.

DICK: Then how?

GWEN: Not all the time. I don't want the responsibility for her life. Not any more.

Enter ERIC.

ERIC: I've found Cleo. About five miles down the road. She's okay.

DICK: I said it was a fuss about nothing.

ERIC: Tied up my tow rope. She's – um – and not in dirt either by the smell of her. I didn't feel I could put her in my car. Not my car. Someone ought to get her.

GWEN: Thank you.

ERIC: Best thing would be for someone to walk her back. Chuck a few sticks in the stream to give her a swim. Shall I give you a lift?

GWEN: I'll get her. I'll get the lead.

ERIC: I'd like to go straight away.

DICK: You coming tomorrow?

ERIC: To pick Jenny up.

DICK: The forecast's good. I thought we could have a walk.

ERIC: Not tomorrow. Maybe next weekend.

DICK: Look forward to it.

GWEN: Shall we go?

ERIC: Heaven knows where she's been. She's not a pretty sight.

They go. As they go JENNY comes out ready to go to work.

DICK: Eric's found her.

GWEN: Eric! Eric! Please stay. She moved. She moved. Please stay.

We hear a car drive off.

Scene Four

The kitchen.
  The acorn still in the bottle is an established plant. DICK enters with ERIC.

DICK: We could have had our walk –

ERIC: Yes –

DICK: You'll have lunch?

ERIC: Yes.

DICK: I've come back to do the veg. The girls are in the pub –

ERIC: I passed the car. Cleo okay?

DICK: Right as rain. Mind you Gwen spent half the morning throwing sticks in the river for her. Don't think she's ever been so clean. Mind if I get on?

ERIC: Go ahead.

DICK puts his apron on.

Anything I can do?

DICK: Sprouts to peel.

ERIC: Fine. Little crosses in the bottom?

DICK: For some reason it does actually make them cook better. Trick Gwen taught me. Sprouts. Colander. And a knife.

ERIC starts to peel sprouts. DICK makes a pudding.

ERIC: Sometimes you wonder if there's any sprout.

DICK: End of season.

Pause.

A problem?

ERIC: Yes.

DICK: Want to talk about it?

ERIC: It'll come out any way.

DICK: Lottie?

ERIC: Yes. I was two hours late to pick her up and this week she wanted to go. She got hysterical as soon as she saw me. I tried to explain that I'd been looking for Cleo so she didn't get run over. It was no good. Nothing I could say was. She told me she never wanted to see me again. She and Linda are going to learn to swim together. There was nothing I could say. Linda had tried her best but two hours! Lottie's furious with Jenny for being pregnant. Me for letting her down. I came away because I didn't know what to say.

DICK: Our fault for expecting you to look.

ERIC: I wasn't looking. I was driving home. There was Cleo in the middle of the road. The last thing I wanted. I was late as it was. I have to spend more time with Lottie. It's all I can do. Stop going away at the weekend so if she wants me to take her swimming I'll be there.

DICK: You can't let a child dictate your life.

ERIC: They do.

DICK: Can't you talk to her?

ERIC: A ten year old. I have to be there for her. It's the only way.

DICK: Bring her with you.

ERIC: It doesn't work between Lottie and Jenny. Up till now it has always been a sort of uneasy truce but since the baby. Lottie wanted to choose the name.

DICK: She's not named yet.

ERIC: For Jenny she is. What Lottie wants is me and Lottie.

DICK: Jealousy. I went through all this with Jenny. Hardly ever in and when she was in wanting all Gwen's time. Wanted to snap her fingers at Gwen. There were times when *I* felt like a stranger. I wanted to leave.

ERIC: Didn't you realise before you married Gwen?

DICK: I thought I could sort it out. Through Gwen to get at Jenny. But Gwen would always say 'She expects it'. And she did. I don't know how she coped when she left. I thought it wasn't serious. That she'd be back with her dirty washing. Did she tell you?

ERIC: A little. Not a time she talks about much.

DICK: And?

ERIC: She moved in with a boy who was at the university.

DICK: We thought at the time she would probably come back pregnant. If she had done I would have thrown her out.

ERIC: Not now?

DICK: Times have changed. I like you. I enjoy your company. I'd prefer you to be married.

ERIC: Stop her staying here Dick. Please. Stop her staying.

DICK: Much better for a child here than in London.

ERIC: I can't come here.

DICK: Commuter belt.

ERIC: Hardly.

DICK: Spend the weekend in London. Weekends –

ERIC: Lottie. It's impossible.

DICK: You have to talk to Jenny.

ERIC: Find an excuse. A reason why she can't stay. Don't make it easy for her.

DICK: Throw her out?

ERIC: Discourage her. The idea of broken nights. Anything – it's too easy for her you see. So easy. Sell her flat and move in here. What could be safer?

DICK: You are as welcome as she is.

ERIC: I have Lottie.

DICK: Build a whole relationship with Jessica.

ERIC: I did with Lottie and look at it.

DICK: Time. Twenty years it's taken me with Jenny. And we're friends now. It's as if we'd never quarrelled. Of course if Lottie means more to you than Jenny.

ERIC: She does that. Half an hour longer with me. Half an hour less with Lottie. Don't let Jenny live here.

DICK: Bring Lottie.

ERIC: The countryside is not a panacea. Linda has custody. Where Lottie is concerned our relationship is good, there's no argument that I should see Lottie more than the two weekends a month I am supposed to be allowed. When she's older she'll get the chance to decide if she wants to live with me. At that stage she'll probably want neither of us.

DICK: Do you think there'll be enough?

ERIC: Yes.

DICK: You could start to lay the table.

ERIC *does so. He now knows his way around the kitchen.*

I'd like to have you here too Eric. Both of you. However you wanted. It's so empty in this house. Gwen always working. Always waiting for her. There soon wouldn't be a foot path we hadn't done. Cleo would love it. Two masters.

The phone rings.

Yes. Yes. He is.

He hands the phone to ERIC.

Your daughter.

ERIC: Lottie? Lottie? It's Daddy.

Scene Five

ERIC *and* JENNY.

JENNY: Don't you want to feel her kicking?

ERIC: No.

JENNY: She moves a lot now. A little acrobat.

ERIC: I don't want to hear.

JENNY: Your child.

ERIC: I don't want any rights.

JENNY: I suppose Gwen'll come with me for the birth.

ERIC: I suppose so.

JENNY: Not even for that?

ERIC: No. That's when I fell in love with Lottie. The sheer perversity to be born. There was a moment when she slithered out and then inflated. The life going into her. Of course financially. A standing order would be best – you could be sure of getting it –

JENNY: She's not a rates demand.

They walk a little.

If I said I'd marry you.

ERIC: No.

JENNY: You asked.

ERIC: I've un-asked.

JENNY: You spoil her.

ERIC: You'll spoil Jessica.

They walk.

There are some of your things at my place. A few records. Clothes.

JENNY: I haven't missed the records. Or the clothes.

ERIC: What would you like me to do with them?

JENNY: Oxfam or a jumble sale I suppose. You won't throw them out in the street or burn them?

ERIC: No. I threw out all Linda's things. You don't do it again. It's not the sort of contingency insurance is designed to cover.

JENNY: Give the clothes to Lottie. She can dress up in them. All the bits of make-up. You should give her all the other bits of eye-shadow and lipstick that have collected under your basin.

ERIC: No one since you.

JENNY: Never?

ERIC: No.

JENNY: Not all the times you left?

ERIC: Why, I come back. Not this time Jenny.

JENNY: No.

DICK *comes out of the house. He carries* ERIC's *wellingtons.*

DICK: You forgot these.

ERIC: Thank you.

DICK: Yes. Well.

ERIC: Wonder when I'll wear them next.

DICK: You'll be welcome here, any time.

ERIC: I know.

DICK: Miss you up on the Downs.

ERIC: Miss walking them.

Pause.

And Cleo. If you're in London.

DICK: Yes.

ERIC: Jenny has my number.

DICK: Good. Give you a ring. Have a drink.

ERIC: All fake log fires around me I'm afraid.

DICK: Well –

ERIC: Thanks.

DICK: Been a nuisance if you'd had to come back for them.

ERIC: All this mud. Have to go in the boot.

DICK: We'll meet in London then?

ERIC: Yes.

DICK: Or here. You don't have to ring. I'm usually about. I'm sorry.

ERIC: I'd better go. You know how quickly the traffic builds up into town.

Pause.

Well – of course in an emergency –

JENNY: Of course.

DICK: I'll hold your hand.

JENNY: I know you will.

ERIC: If there's anything else –

DICK: We'll send a parcel.

ERIC: I did think I'd checked. I'm usually pretty methodical.

JENNY: Give Lottie my love.

ERIC: I'm sure she sends hers.

JENNY: Yes.

ERIC *goes.*

I'm cold.

DICK: Stupid to be out here without a coat.

JENNY: It looked warm.

DICK: Still only April. Best time of year up on the Downs. Things beginning

He starts to go.

Come in. You won't see him wave from here.

Scene Six

The office. A coffee machine has appeared; JENNY *is working at* GWEN's *desk. Enter* GWEN.

GWEN: I do hate going round houses, left with their furniture and fittings and no-one there. I don't know how people can bear to leave their lives like that.

JENNY: Aren't they dead?

GWEN: Not always. Pack their bags and go. Send instructions to sell.

JENNY: News for you.

GWEN: Yes?

JENNY: Briar Cottage.

GWEN: What?

JENNY: Fifteen hundred on the offer. Cash. No strings.

GWEN: Have they had a survey?

JENNY: Seeing is believing.

GWEN: Not with a house.

JENNY: Fifteen hundred more. Aren't you impressed?

JENNY: But the Garrads?

JENNY: If they want the property they'll have to match it.

GWEN: They can't.

JENNY: There we are then.

GWEN: Jenny no one should have looked at it. It's under offer.

JENNY: Exactly what these people wanted. And no strings. Money on the table.

GWEN: It was under offer.

JENNY: Do be realistic.

GWEN: The Garrads' offer had been accepted.

JENNY: It's been unaccepted.

GWEN: You shouldn't have sent anyone to see it.

JENNY: Fifteen hundred pounds.

GWEN: It's not the way I do business.

JENNY: It's no wonder you're stuck with one office is it? Throwing away commission.

GWEN: As far as I'm concerned that house is the Garrads'.

JENNY: The new offer has been accepted.

GWEN: It shouldn't have been offered.

JENNY: Well it has been and in fairness to our clients.

GWEN: Have you asked the Garrads if they can match it?

JENNY: We know they can't. Look at the scrabble they've had for a mortgage.

GWEN: But they've been offered one.

JENNY: The principle's established. If the building society can commit to one house for them they can commit to another.

GWEN: They don't want anywhere else.

JENNY: Then they'll have to change their minds. You're silly to fall in love with a house.

GWEN: You can't do it.

JENNY: I have done. The sellers have accepted. Needless to say they're delighted. It means they'll be able to afford upstairs carpets.

GWEN: You can't do it.

JENNY: The new deposit is in the safe.

GWEN: Get it out and give it them back.

JENNY: Look this happens all the time.

GWEN: Not here.

JENNY: Oh come on mother. The real world.

GWEN: It's Dutch auction.

JENNY: A better offer was received and has been accepted.

GWEN: On whose authority?

JENNY: My own.

GWEN: You have no rights here.

JENNY: Our partnership.

GWEN: What partnership?

JENNY: We agreed.

GWEN: I have never agreed.

JENNY: Jenny you can take this client and show them round. Can you go to Woolworths and get keys cut?

GWEN: You offered.

JENNY: You knew on what terms.

GWEN: They weren't accepted.

JENNY: Of course they were. Why go on using me?

GWEN: I haven't used you.

JENNY: Dogsbody.

GWEN: I thought you wanted to learn?

JENNY: I have learnt.

GWEN: Nothing.

JENNY: I got a thousand pounds more for my flat than I dreamed I would. Now this.

GWEN: I don't do business that way.

JENNY: Then what are you doing here?

GWEN: I'm successful.

JENNY: In whose terms?

GWEN: My own.

JENNY: Then aim higher. Push.

GWEN: I don't need to.

JENNY: You've never thought of it.

GWEN: My word. People trust my word. Buyers come here because they know they won't be gazumped.

JENNY: Then it's the sellers who are fools.

GWEN: A lot of people wanting to buy means a lot of sales.

JENNY: I know you started this business as a game but it's real now.

GWEN: It's always been real since I ordered the notepaper and envelopes.

JENNY: There's more to business than stationery.

GWEN: Yes and I've given it.

JENNY: You might have got a better return on your investment.

GWEN: We are quite comfortable. We have two cars. In my childhood I thought people with bicycles were the aristocracy. I didn't dare dream of a bicycle.

JENNY: Then dream now.

GWEN: What of?

JENNY: Whatever you want. Why settle for comfort?

GWEN: What is there after that?

JENNY: The icing on the cake. A little luxury. Why do I have to sleep on sheets that have joins down the centre?

GWEN: My wedding sheets.

JENNY: You divorced him.

Pause.

GWEN: Briar Cottage belongs to the Garrads.

JENNY: They can't afford it.

GWEN: They can.

JENNY: How?

GWEN: I'll find them the money.

JENNY: Where?

GWEN: My bank account if necessary.

JENNY: St. Joan?

GWEN: I gave my word the house was theirs. I promised.

JENNY: A final offer has been made and accepted.

GWEN: The Garrads' was the final offer.

JENNY: A better final offer.

GWEN: I'll give you a better final final offer. An extra two thousand.

Pause.

It's good business Jenny. I'll match you all the way.

JENNY: What if the Garrads don't want your beneficence?

GWEN: Buy it myself. Sell it them at a price they can afford.

JENNY: Cash?

GWEN: Pound notes on the table if you like.

JENNY: What would you do with a cottage?

GWEN: Live in it. Or perhaps you could go there with your baby. The one that isn't going to cry in the night. I'd forgotten. You've thrown up your job you'll have all day to catch up on your sleep.

JENNY: You promised. A deal. I've sold my flat.

GWEN: It was voices St. Joan heard wasn't it?

JENNY: I've come back.

GWEN: You've gone once. You can go again.

JENNY: Where?

GWEN: Oxford. Throw your keys in the river. No – one thing you might have learned is keys are expensive. I'd rather you gave them back.

Scene Seven

The kitchen.
    Early morning.
    GWEN *looking at the tapestry on the frame. It is all but finished.*
    Enter DICK.

DICK: You making tea?

GWEN: If you like.

She plugs in the kettle.

DICK: Up early.

GWEN: Couldn't sleep.

DICK: You should stop worrying.

GWEN: How?

DICK: Relax more. Once Jessica's born and Jenny's back at work –

GWEN: Come home and change nappies.

DICK: I'll do that.

GWEN: Six or seven times a day for two and a half years?

DICK: It will be fun.

GWEN: For how long?

About the tapestry.

Nearly finished.

DICK: Yes. Promised it to Jenny.

GWEN: Jenny?

DICK: When she first came she liked it. I said I'd give it to her.

GWEN: It's for the dining chair.

DICK: I can do another. I have the time.

GWEN: Can't she wait?

DICK: I said she could have it.

GWEN: It's one of a set. Doesn't she realise?

DICK: Another one. It's easy enough.

GWEN: Let her wait her turn.

DICK: I told her she could have it. Makes a change. Your making tea for me.

GWEN: Do you hate it so much?

DICK: I do it for you.

GWEN: Do you hate it?

DICK: I do it gladly.

GWEN: Then why do you want me back here?

DICK: You're not so young as you were. You work crazy hours. I want us to spend time together.

GWEN: With Jenny here?

DICK: She'll make her own friends. Be out all the time.

GWEN: And we babysit.

DICK: It's what grandmothers are for.

GWEN: Not this one.

DICK: You can't throw her out.

GWEN: It's going to be her or me Dick. In the end.

DICK: You haven't slept. Come back to bed.

GWEN: No. I mean it.

DICK: Yes. Yes.

GWEN: Yes.

DICK: She'll get sick of us soon enough. Find a place of her own.

GWEN: We're too convenient.

DICK: Wait until after the baby.

GWEN: And throw a mother and child out on the streets.

DICK: Oxfordshire is hardly the streets.

GWEN: As soon as I saw her I knew she wanted something.

DICK: You've always given into her before.

GWEN: Not this time.

DICK: Any digestives?

GWEN: Did you buy any?

DICK: No.

GWEN: Then there aren't.

DICK: Jenny sometimes gets some. She likes one with her tea.

GWEN *looks in the tin. There are digestive biscuits in it.* DICK *lays a tray for* JENNY.

GWEN: A cup of tea with a biscuit in the saucer.

DICK: I like to do it properly for her.

GWEN: She's hardly a guest.

DICK (*goes back to the table and pours*): Have this argument with her. Not with me.

GWEN: The two of you thick as thieves.

DICK: You can't expect us not to talk.

GWEN: You didn't used to.

DICK: We have a lot in common.

GWEN: What?

DICK: You.

GWEN: Her or me Dick.

DICK: You make it sound like an ultimatum..

GWEN: It is.

DICK: We'll sit down all of us and talk.

GWEN: With her there?

DICK: Something has to be sorted out. It can't go on like this.

GWEN: Send her away.

DICK: Your daughter. You do it.

Pause.

GWEN: How?

DICK: How ever you do.

GWEN: But she might go for good.

DICK: The risk you'll take –

GWEN: That I couldn't bear but this –

DICK: Tea –

GWEN: No.

DICK: Biscuit –

GWEN: No. I'm going to sell the business.

DICK: Pardon?

GWEN: Sell it. Unencumber myself.

DICK: Jenny's job.

GWEN: What job? I've never given her one.

DICK: She works for you.

GWEN: For herself. The pound signs ticking up behind her eyeballs.

DICK: You don't have to sell it if you want to retire.

GWEN: I don't want to retire. I won't work with her.

DICK: Find her a job somewhere else.

GWEN: Pull strings.

DICK: Your own child it's natural.

GWEN: At her age? What would they think of me? Or her? Her own mother can't work with her?

DICK: Wait until after the baby.

GWEN: Wait? What for?

DICK: You'll love the baby when you see her. You'll love her.

GWEN: It's isn't like that. It doesn't happen in that way. They're dependent. That's what's attractive about babies. The

power you have over them.

DICK: Maternal instinct.

GWEN: Aching breasts and passion poured down an empty hole.

DICK: Bonding.

GWEN: A gamble. The stock exchange.

DICK: You have no rights.

GWEN: Does she?

DICK: You chose to have her.

GWEN: I wanted him not her. I didn't think about her. Him doing his duty. Me in a white dress. Look what I've ended up with.

DICK: Me and Jenny.

GWEN: Do you think this is your child to make up?

DICK: In a way. I've never held a baby Gwen. Just a pile of bloody sheets. She's asked me to go with her to the hospital. Nowadays a loving partner is all they specify.

GWEN: Will you go? Screaming. All that blood?

DICK: I can hold her hand.

GWEN: She didn't even ask me.

DICK: We thought you'd be working.

He picks up the tray.

GWEN: I'll take Cleo out. Let her sniff at the primroses.

DICK: Good.

GWEN: Dick –

DICK: Yes?

GWEN: I tried for you.

DICK: You didn't have to.

GWEN: But I did.

DICK *goes.*
GWEN *cuts the tapestry from the frame and puts it in her brief case.*
She takes the oak tree from the glass.
She takes Cleo's lead and dog bowl.
She takes her key from the key ring and leaves it on the table.
She goes.

Scene Eight

The wood.
   The moments before dawn.
   Enter GWEN.
   She is dressed as in the first scene, smart
with her briefcase.
   She carries the oak tree.
   She plants it, using her hands to dig.
   She crosses the stage and looks back at the
house.
   She crosses the stage and goes.
   She whistles for Cleo.
   Dawn breaks.